EDGAR ALLAN POE

TOM STREISSGUTH

In Consultation with Martha Cosgrove,
M.A. and Reading Specialist

LERNER PUBLICATIONS COMPANY / MINNEAPOLIS

Martha Cosgrove has a master's degree from the University of Minnesota in secondary education, with an emphasis on developmental and remedial reading. She is licensed in 7–12 English and language arts, developmental reading, and remedial reading. She has had several works published, and she gives numerous state and national presentations in her areas of expertise.

Lerner Publications Company
A division of Lerner Publishing Group
241 First Avenue North
Minneapolis, Minnesota 55401 U.S.A.

Website address: www.lernerbooks.com

Library of Congress Cataloging-in-Publication Data

Streissguth, Thomas, 1958-
    Edgar Allan Poe / by Tom Streissguth.
        p.   cm. — (Just the facts biographies)
    Includes bibliographical references and index.
    ISBN-13: 978-0-8225-6800-1 (lib. bdg. : alk. paper)
    ISBN-10: 0-8225-6800-4 (lib. bdg. : alk. paper)
    1. Poe, Edgar Allan, 1809-1849–Juvenile literature.   2. Authors,
American–19th century–Biography–Juvenile literature.   I. Title.
PS2631.S86 2007
818'.309–dc22 [B]   2006018984

Manufactured in the United States of America
1 2 3 4 5 6 – DP – 12 11 10 09 08 07

CONTENTS

1

ORPHANED

EDGAR ALLAN POE'S STORY "The Black Cat" was first published on August 19, 1843. He had become famous for his thrilling short stories. Here's part of the story:

> No sooner had the [sound] of my blows sunk into silence than I was answered by a voice from within the tomb!—by a cry, . . . like the sobbing of a child, and then quickly swelling into one long, loud, and continuous scream . . . a wailing shriek,

half of horror and half of triumph, such as
might have arisen only out of hell. . . .
[Then I saw] the corpse, already greatly
decayed and clotted with gore. . . . Upon
its head . . . sat the [cat] whose craft had
seduced me into murder.

Edgar Poe was thirty-four years old and poor.
He lived in a small house in Philadelphia,
Pennsylvania. By the 1840s, he had written many
stories such as "The Black Cat." In many of his
works, he created creepy situations. He hoped his
writings would scare his readers.

Edgar had had his share of unhappy and scary
moments. His father, David Poe, had disappeared
in early 1810, when Edgar was not yet two years
old. His mother, a beautiful actress named Eliza
Poe, died in December 1810. She left her young
children—William, Edgar, and Rosalie—to make their
way in the world as orphans.

ARRIVING IN THE UNITED STATES

Poe's mother was eight years old when she arrived
in the United States from Great Britain in 1795.
Her stage career began on April 15, 1796, in

Eliza Poe, Edgar's mother

Boston, Massachusetts. Over the next ten years, she played sweet girls, tough girls, and lovesick women. She could sing and dance. She could memorize long, difficult speaking parts. She appeared in plays all along the East Coast of the United States. Critics praised her acting. Her soft voice brought her attention and applause. The public loved her long, dark hair and her large, dark eyes.

When Eliza was about eighteen, she married an actor named Charles Hopkins. But on October 26, 1805, Hopkins died of yellow

It's a Fact!

Both Poe's mother and grandmother were successful stage actresses.

fever. Eliza then met David Poe, a gentleman from Baltimore, Maryland. David Poe had once been a lawyer. He had left his career to become an actor. Unfortunately, he had a bad case of stage fright. His awkward speaking voice often drew hisses from audiences. The critics thought he was a very bad actor.

In April 1806, Eliza married David Poe. Life was hard. Money was very short for Mr. and Mrs. Poe. The theater company they worked for tried to help them. Sometimes the company gave the Poes all the money it earned from benefit performances. Even though they didn't have much money, the Poes started a family. On January

An announcement for the *Curfew*. This was one of the benefit performances that helped David and Eliza Poe get extra money for their family.

30, 1807, Eliza gave birth to William Henry. The family didn't have enough money to care for the baby. So the couple decided to give their son to David Poe's parents, who were better off. On January 19, 1809, Edgar Poe was born. The family was in Boston, at the time.

THE POE FAMILY

Desperately poor, David Poe begged for a few dollars from a wealthy cousin, George Poe. George thought his cousin was worthless. He refused to give David any money. Eliza and David fought about their money problems. In early 1810, David Poe disappeared. Eliza continued to act in New York, Boston, and Virginia to make money. Eliza's friends and people who liked her acting gave her money, food, and clothing. Their gifts eased the family's poverty. To make matters worse, Eliza was pregnant again. She and Edgar were in Virginia.

During the following months, Eliza slowly lost her health. She came down with tuberculosis. At this time, this serious lung disease could not be cured. On December 20, 1810, she gave birth to Rosalie.

Several ladies of Richmond helped Eliza in her last months. One of them, Frances "Fanny" Allan.

She was the wife of a wealthy Richmond merchant named John Allan. The Allans had enjoyed many of Eliza's performances. Fanny wanted to help the actress who had entertained her so well. She brought warm clothing, food, and medicine to Eliza's sickroom. Even with all the help she received, Eliza could not get better. In late December, she died quietly, with her children around her.

A DISTANT FATHER

After Eliza's death, Fanny Allan wrote to David Poe's parents in Baltimore. They were already taking care of William Henry. Fanny offered to take Edgar. She would take care of him and make sure

John Allan   Fanny Allan

he got an education. Another rich family in Richmond offered to care for Rosalie. The Poe family agreed.

Edgar had started his life in crowded rooms. After his mother died, he moved to the Allans' big, warm house in Richmond. He had books to read and a yard to play in. He stayed in a room of his own. The Allans also took trips in horse-drawn carriages out of Richmond. They visited the beautiful Shenandoah Valley and the Blue Ridge Mountains.

But John Allan had little time to spend with his foster son. Instead, Allan spent most of his time in his office. He bought and sold tobacco, leather,

Edgar lived in Richmond, Virginia *(above)*, with the Allans.

wine, food, and land. He was also coping with the War of 1812 (1812–1815) against Great Britain. The war had hurt Allan's international business. After the war, the United States was again trading freely with countries across the Atlantic Ocean. Allan was busy arranging purchases, sales, and shipments. He didn't have much time for a young boy who was not even related to him.

WAR OF 1812

The War of 1812 *(below)* actually lasted almost three years. Nearly thirty years earlier, the young United States had won its independence from Britain. But Britain wasn't treating the United States like a self-ruling country. In the early 1800s, British ships attacked U.S. ships. The British took away U.S. sailors and forced them to serve in the British navy. The United States declared war on Britain in June of 1812. Business and trade suffered during the war. Neither goods nor supplies could get through to customers.

Forces from both nations fought at sea and on land. British troops even set fire to Washington, D.C., the new U.S. capital. Eventually, the United States won. By 1815, a treaty had settled the conflict. As a result, trade started up again, and John Allan's businesses recovered. Edgar was again able to enjoy the benefits of being part of a wealthy family.

CHAPTER 2
MOVING AROUND

This picture of young Edgar was taken when he was about five years old.

IN 1815, JOHN ALLAN OPENED an office in London, England. The family moved there and rented a house. Mr. Allan sent six-year-old Edgar to a boarding school. Two years later, Allan sent Edgar to the Manor House in central England. At Manor House, Edgar went by the name of Edgar Allan. He was eight years old and very thin. Yet Edgar was still strong enough to walk for miles in the surrounding countryside.

John Allan paid all of Edgar's expenses. He gave him the best education possible. Allan's homes always held many books. At this time, books were too expensive for most families to own. Allan wrote Edgar many letters. He told the young boy to study hard and to stay out of trouble. The students learned foreign languages, poetry, math, and religion. Edgar did well in school.

Most of the time, Edgar was outgoing and friendly. But sometimes he got depressed and felt homesick. John Allan was in London, taking care of his business. Fanny Allan paid little attention to Edgar. To relieve his loneliness, Edgar turned to books. He especially liked the tales and poetry of Lord Byron. In Byron's works, brave men overcame danger by being noble and courageous. Byron's heroes didn't fear death.

Edgar also came to like the works of the German poet Johann Wolfgang von Goethe. He discovered the British poets Percy Shelley and William Wordsworth. These three poets wrote about love, fear, courage, and the beauty of nature. They were part of the Romantic movement of writers. These writers rejected the cold reason and strict logic that had been popular in the 1700s.

ROMANTIC MOVEMENT VS. THE AGE OF REASON

The Romantic movement touched both writing and the arts in the 1800s. The Romantic style stressed passion, the beauty of nature, and individual freedoms. It rejected reason and logic. These ideas were part of the Age of Reason of the 1700s. Romantic writers chose topics in folklore, ancient history, and even the supernatural. Edgar Allan Poe—with his passionate personality and his supernatural writing—was a symbol of the Romantic movement.

TROUBLE IN RICHMOND

John Allan's business in London thrived until 1819. In that year, the demand for American tobacco fell. Unable to sell his goods in Europe, Allan nearly went bankrupt (had to declare he couldn't pay his debts). In 1820, after five years in Britain, the family again crossed the Atlantic Ocean. This time, John Allan had only a little money in his pocket. His family was poor. Its future was uncertain.

In Richmond, Virginia, John Allan moved his family into cheap lodgings. He tried to settle his many debts. Edgar studied in small schools run by tutors. He was able to easily read the works of ancient Roman poets. Their works were originally written in Latin. Edgar became skilled at reading this ancient language.

He also felt a strong admiration for military life. In 1824, when he was fifteen, Edgar volunteered for the Junior Morgan Riflemen of Richmond. He proudly wore the riflemen's uniform. He led parades and marches whenever he had the chance.

Gradually, Allan recovered from his business troubles. Then, in 1825, he inherited the huge sum of $750,000 (nearly $13 million in modern money) from his uncle. John Allan became one of the wealthiest men in Richmond. People both respected and envied him.

Allan's business also thrived. The merchants of Richmond were profiting from a time of peace in the United States. There were no more wars against Britain. Bitter rivalries among different political parties in Washington, D.C., faded into the past. New machines allowed new factories to do well. At the same time, the United States was expanding westward.

AN EXCELLENT STUDENT

Edgar paid little attention to his foster father's money or his business. The boy still suffered from

loneliness. Most of the time, he felt unwanted. He
started using "Allan" as his middle name. After
all, John Allan had never legally adopted him.
Edgar realized that many people didn't consider
him a real part of the Allan family. He felt
embarrassed by this uncertain status. He grew
quiet and sullen. He began to withdraw from John
and Fanny Allan.

Even so, sixteen-year-old Edgar was still eager
to study and learn. He could read Latin and
French easily. He particularly enjoyed the works of
literary masters such as the French playwright
Molière. He dreamed of writing poetry as good as
that of Lord Byron. He spent his evenings at a
small desk in his room, writing poetry and plays.
He also wrote stories that made fun of familiar
Richmond characters, especially merchants. In a
way, his stories made fun of his foster father. At
one point, he had written enough plays and poems
to make a book. He asked John Allan to help him
get the book published. Allan refused. He didn't
want Edgar to get a big head by seeing his own
name in print.

In school, Edgar was competitive. He wanted
to do well at everything. He excelled at reading

and writing in foreign languages. His slender but athletic body allowed him to shine at sports. He could run quickly, box skillfully, and swim strongly. He loved to overcome challenges and to show off.

In the fall of 1825, Edgar's brother, William Henry Poe, came from Baltimore to visit him. Together they visited their sister, Rosalie. That same fall, Edgar met and quickly fell in love with a Richmond girl, Sarah Elmira Royster. The two began to talk of marriage.

An artist's drawing of Sarah Elmira Royster as a teenager

UNIVERSITY OF VIRGINIA

In February 1826, John Allan sent seventeen-year-old Edgar to the University of Virginia in Charlottesville. According to Allan, a university education would give Edgar a good start in life. He expected Edgar to go into business. In turn, Allan would look like a generous foster father. Allan gave Edgar a bit of spending money. He also warned him to study hard.

THE UNIVERSITY OF VIRGINIA

The University of Virginia *(below)* first opened its doors in 1825. Founding Father Thomas Jefferson had personally designed the campus. He even put together the first courses. Jefferson invited students to dinner at nearby Monticello, his large home. Edgar was lucky enough to be one of them.

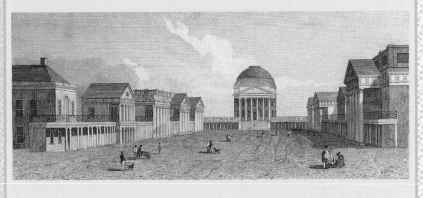

At the university, Edgar read the works of French and Italian writers. He earned praise for translating Latin poetry. The poetry of Lord Byron, Percy Shelley, and others filled his evening hours. Their works inspired him to write more verse. He recited his poems for his classmates. They admired his skill at writing poetry on any subject.

But Edgar earned nothing from his writings. He couldn't pay for the expenses of student life with the money Allan had given him. The seventeen-year-old ran into serious debt for his clothing and his books. Edgar also started drinking and gambling at cards. He usually lost. He had to borrow money from classmates to pay his debts.

Edgar soon discovered that university life wasn't all peaceful study and good times. Fights and riots broke out among students. Students often cheated on their exams. Many of them became roaring drunk at night. They threatened and sometimes attacked their professors.

Edgar also felt abandoned. Edgar often wrote to Sarah Royster. But she wasn't answering any of his letters. She was still young—only fifteen years old. Her father opposed the idea of an engagement between Sarah and Edgar. Unknown to Edgar, Mr.

Royster destroyed his letters before they could reach his daughter.

Edgar returned to Richmond after one year at the university. John Allan refused to give him any more money for his education. He would not allow Edgar to harm his family's reputation with gambling, drinking, and money trouble.

LEAVING HOME

Although he admired good writing, John Allan would not support Edgar's dream to be a poet. Allan believed Edgar needed discipline. He wanted him to go into business.

Edgar agreed to work in John Allan's office. But Edgar knew before he started that he wasn't made for the routines of business. His business was poetry. He longed to explore his feelings with words. A bitterness grew between Edgar and John Allan. On March 19, 1827, they had a terrible argument. Edgar was irresponsible, said his foster father. He was arrogant, wasteful, and idle. His behavior had been self-centered and demanding. Allan was self-righteous and cold, replied Edgar. He was cheap and did not feel any love for his family.

After the long and angry talk, Edgar stormed away. Without looking back, Edgar walked across the porch, down the steps, and into the streets of Richmond. He carried nothing but the clothes on his back.

From a tavern in central Richmond, Edgar wrote a letter to John Allan. He knew he would never win Allan's affection. This letter would mark an important new direction. He believed that he was about to enter the real world. He thought the public would show him respect. He would finally earn glory and fame. Here's part of the letter:

After my treatment of yesterday and what passed between us this morning, I can hardly think you will be surprised at the contents of this letter. My determination is . . . to leave your house and [try] to find some place in this wide world, where I will be treated—not as you have treated me. . . . Send my trunk etc. to the Court-house Tavern, send me . . . some money immediately—as I am in the greatest necessity.

Yours etc.

Edgar A Poe

John Allan was right about one thing, however. Edgar was a very stubborn young man. He would not give in. He would live the way he wanted. Allan didn't answer Edgar's letter. He sent no money. He didn't deliver Edgar's trunk of clothes. From this time forward, his eighteen-year-old foster son would be on his own.

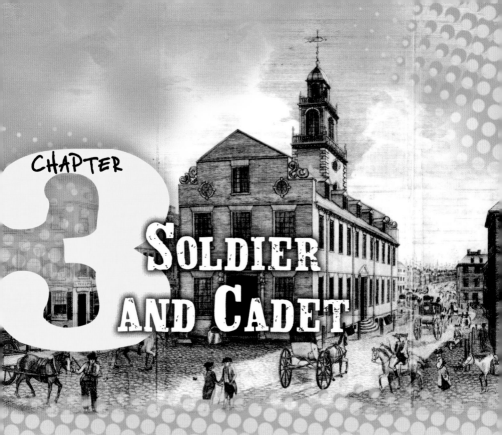

CHAPTER 3
SOLDIER AND CADET

EDGAR CHOSE TO LEAVE Richmond and move to Boston. He spent many lonely months there. He couldn't find work. He couldn't sell the poetry he had written. He lived on money he borrowed from friends.

Edgar felt ashamed of his miserable life. He created stories about himself. He even gave himself a new name—Henri le Rennert. He spread tales of his adventures in Russia. He said he'd had adventures at sea. He told people he'd fought bravely against the Turks, whom the Greeks were fighting in the 1820s.

Edgar moved to Boston, Massachusetts *(above)*, in April 1827.

23

IN THE ARMY NOW

In May 1827, Edgar turned himself into a real soldier. He joined the U.S. Army. He felt certain this career would be truly exciting. In addition, he'd have a comfortable bed and steady meals. Edgar was weak from many months of hunger and poverty. He feared the army recruiters might not want him. But he showed them his self-confidence. The recruiters accepted him. He gave his name as Edgar Perry and his age as twenty-two (he was actually eighteen). The army sent him to the First Artillery Regiment at Fort Independence, in Boston.

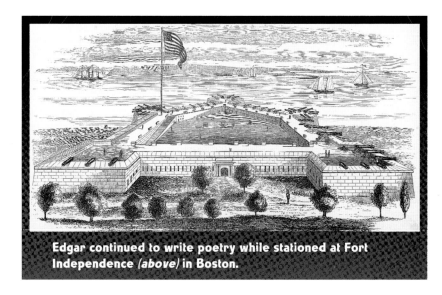

Edgar continued to write poetry while stationed at Fort Independence (*above*) in Boston.

Military service did not stop Edgar from writing poetry or from trying to publish his works. He gave his feelings of loneliness a clear voice. He still looked to Byron and Shelley as his models. But he also began to develop his own style. In his writing, he explored the difference between reality and dreams. The power of his imagination to reshape the world fascinated him. He wanted the words and the lines he wrote to have a powerful effect on his readers.

Not long after Edgar joined the army, a small booklet titled *Tamerlane and Other Poems* appeared in Boston's bookshops. The author's name was simply "A Bostonian." In fact, the Bostonian was Edgar. He had given the poems to a young printer named

IT'S A FACT!

Genghis Khan lived in the late 1100s and the early 1200s. He came from central Asia, where he was the leader of the Mongols. Eventually, the Mongols ruled much of Asia. Tamerlane claimed to be Genghis's grandson. He was born in 1336 near Samarqand in what would later become Uzbekistan. He took control of parts of Russia, India, and much of western Asia. His rule was harsh, but he was also known as a man of learning.

Calvin F. S. Thomas. Thomas had agreed to publish this collection. "Tamerlane," the title poem, tells the story of a great Asian soldier. He was a descendant of Genghis Khan, the Mongol war leader. In the poem, Tamerlane looks back on the sacrifices he has made to reach his dreams.

In the army, Edgar worked hard. He followed orders and stayed out of trouble. His officers noticed his intelligence and hard work. They promoted him to assistant commissary. This rank made him responsible for the regiment's food supplies. On January 1, 1829, Edgar won another promotion, to sergeant major. It was the highest rank he could reach as an enlisted soldier. (He was not in line to become an officer.)

It's a Fact!

A commissary is the storehouse for food and other goods at a military camp. The word also refers to the person in charge of the commissary's supplies.

New Directions

Edgar had enlisted in the army for a five-year term. But within two years, he was ready to leave. He believed he had learned enough self-discipline to

last him a lifetime. And the army didn't need him.
The United States wasn't at war with anyone. In
fact, the United States hadn't been in a war since
the War of 1812.

Edgar went to Colonel William Drayton, an
officer as well as a friend. Edgar asked to break his
enlistment before his term was finished. Colonel
Drayton agreed on two conditions. Edgar must
make up with his foster father. And his foster father
must give his consent.

Edgar agreed and wrote a letter to John Allan.
In the letter, he claimed to be more grown up. The
army couldn't help him anymore. He said he was
ready to make his own way in the world.

Allan didn't answer Edgar's letter. Edgar wrote
again and then a third time. He tried a new
strategy. He asked Allan to help him enter the
military academy at West Point. This was the U.S.
Army's college. There, Edgar could prepare to
become an officer. Edgar saw officer training as
more useful than an enlistment as a common
soldier. He believed this might finally convince
Allan to help him.

Then Edgar heard the news that Fanny Allan
had died. He took a leave of absence and returned

to John Allan's home. In honor of Fanny's memory, Allan and Edgar put aside their differences. Allan agreed to sponsor Edgar's enrollment at West Point.

On April 15, 1829, the U.S. Army discharged Edgar. For his application to West Point, three officers wrote letters of support. Allan also asked for help from rich Virginia citizens. With these letters, Edgar won a place on a waiting list of candidates for West Point.

While waiting, twenty-year-old Edgar moved to Baltimore. There he arranged for the publication of another book of poetry, *Al Aaraaf.* The publisher– Carey, Lea, and Carey of Philadelphia–asked Edgar for the money to print the book. As payment Edgar would earn only a few copies of the book. Edgar still had no money. So he asked for John Allan's help in paying for the publication. John Allan

IT'S A FACT!

"Al Aaraaf" is the unusual title of one of Edgar's early poems. It comes from an Arabic word—*al-a'raf*, or "dividing line"—that appears in the Quran, the Islamic holy book. The word refers to an area between heaven and hell, a sort of limbo. In this place, departed souls await their chance to become pure in spirit.

angrily refused. He believed there was no future in being a poet.

Edgar managed to arrange to have the book published anyway. That November, his poetry appeared under the true name of Edgar A. Poe in a volume titled *Al Aaraaf, Tamerlane, and Minor Poems.* Critics in Boston and Baltimore reviewed the book. Some of the reviews were positive. Some were negative. Still, Edgar had achieved an important goal. Critics, booksellers, and a few readers finally knew his name.

At West Point

In the spring of 1830, Edgar became a cadet (student) at West Point. That summer, he and the other cadets lived outdoors on the academy's grounds. He spent mornings marching and attending classes. In the afternoons, he studied and marched some more. The exercise and outdoor life brought Edgar good health. He grew stronger. He took classes in math and French. He wrote poetry when he had the time.

The officers of West Point scheduled every minute of Edgar's day. They said when he would go to bed and when he would get up. The other

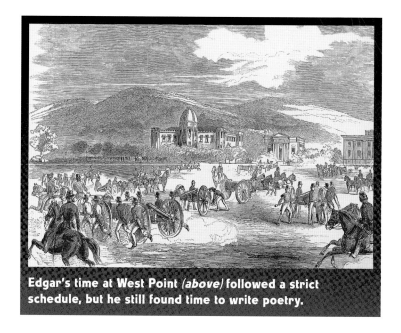

Edgar's time at West Point *(above)* followed a strict schedule, but he still found time to write poetry.

cadets surrounded him like a big family. Edgar enjoyed the discipline. But he also enjoyed breaking the rules. On occasion, the cadets secretly drank, gambled, and fought. Edgar felt as though he were taking part in a great adventure. For a time, he felt content.

Then Edgar received the news that John Allan had remarried. Allan's second wife was named Louisa Patterson. The wedding took place not far from West Point. John Allan had not invited his foster son to the wedding. Louisa had known Edgar as a boy. She thought he was stubborn. She didn't like him. Shortly after the wedding, Allan wrote a final letter to Edgar. He asked that his foster son stop writing him.

The letter threw Edgar into a deep depression. He felt himself cut off from his family and his boyhood in Richmond. He felt alone. He could not see a future for himself. In some down moments, he thought he might never find his way in the world.

Early in 1831, Edgar decided to quit West Point. He had been there only a year. Once again, he had to write to John Allan. Allan had to give his consent for Edgar to leave the military. In the letter, Edgar poured out his bitter feelings.

Allan didn't reply. Without his foster father's help, Edgar had no way to leave West Point. He had to get himself thrown out. He began breaking as many rules as he could. He missed classes and earned bad grades. His behavior got him in trouble. Finally, the commanding officer called for a court-martial—a trial for a member of the military.

The court charged Edgar with neglect of duty and of his studies. Edgar admitted that he was guilty. The academy dismissed him. He paid the money due for his clothing, books, and room and board.

IT'S A FACT!

To get a full release from the army, Poe had to pay for someone to replace him.

With the little money he had left, he returned to civilian life.

Edgar made his way to New York. He decided to start fresh there. Despite his troubles, he felt hopeful for the future. His poetry had been published in Boston and in Baltimore. Another edition of his works would appear soon. One-dollar donations from 131 of his West Point classmates paid for the publication. The book might finally bring him fame and fortune. Then again, it might attract no attention at all. Few people in the United States had

Edgar wrote the poem "Alone" (right) shortly after he left West Point. The poem tells of his sadness at being alone in the world.

money to spend on poetry books. Fewer still would pay for the creations of an unknown young man. But Edgar felt sure of one thing. He would find the glory he deserved as a poet, not as a military man.

CHAPTER 4

BALTIMORE FAMILY

Maria Clemm *(above)* provided a much-needed home for Edgar.

TWENTY-TWO-YEAR-OLD EDGAR POE had no money. He wandered penniless through Boston and New York until the spring of 1831. Then he moved to Baltimore. He went to live with his aunt, Maria Clemm. She was David Poe's sister. Four others lived with her—her son, Henry; her daughter, Virginia; Edgar's brother, William Henry Poe; and Edgar's grandmother, Elizabeth Poe.

Maria was a tall, kind, and practical woman. Eight-year-old Virginia had dark eyes and long, black hair. Even as a young girl, the paleness of her skin and her large eyes gave her a faraway look.

Maria and Virginia admired Edgar. He was handsome. His manners were those of a gentleman. His eyes held the attention of those he met. He had a poetic way of speaking.

To provide for themselves, Maria and Virginia usually relied on family and friends. Edgar felt proud to have the new responsibility of supporting them. He was happy that he was no longer alone in the world. He wrote letters to the editors of the dozens of magazines in Baltimore. He wrote

Edgar's young cousin, Virginia

to schools, hoping to find a teaching job. All his letters were politely rejected.

FIRST SHORT STORIES

Edgar's failure to find a job began to eat away at his self-confidence. Then, on August 1, 1831, his brother died after years of sickness. Edgar became the sole provider for the household. He had to find some way to raise money. Meanwhile, he had read about a contest in the *Philadelphia Saturday Courier*. The paper would award $100 (about $2,000 in modern money) for the best short story. The contest inspired Edgar to try writing stories. He worked hard and soon finished five tales.

Edgar didn't win the prize. But the *Courier*'s editors liked his stories. The next year, they

Edgar lived in this Baltimore home with the Clemms.

published all of them. On January 14, 1832, one of the stories, "Metzengerstein," became Edgar's first published story.

Edgar saw a new career. He could write stories that could win him fame and fortune. Poetry inspired deep feelings in readers. But stories could also have a strong effect. His stories could terrify people. His mysteries could give a view of strange, unknown worlds. His readers would remember his words, if he chose them well.

Edgar worked hard. In the spring of 1833, he finished an entire collection of stories called *Eleven Tales of the Arabesque*. In the book, the members of the Folio Club tell tales and then discuss them. They talk about what was good about them and what didn't work.

EDGAR AND THE SHORT STORY

For hundreds of years, the most popular works of fiction have been novels. A novel is simply a very long story. Edgar wrote short stories and poetry. Why?

Poe always worked and thought like a poet. He wanted people to admire the beauty of his words and his skill at choosing them. He wanted readers to laugh, to cry, or to be terrified. To him, novels had too many characters. The plots in such a long work can be complex. With the short story, Edgar could skillfully create a mood with a few well-chosen lines. He was constantly interested in that challenge.

On June 13, 1833, the *Baltimore Saturday Visiter* announced a writing contest. The editors would award $50 (about $1,000) for the best tale and $25 (about $500) for the best poem. Edgar sent the *Visiter* six of his new stories, as well as a new poem, "The Coliseum." On October 12, the *Visiter* announced the short-story winner: Edgar's "MS. [manuscript] Found in a Bottle." The newspaper published it one week later. The story describes a ship that goes through a terrifying storm at sea. The narrator, a passenger, talks about his final moments before he dies.

With "MS. Found in a Bottle," Edgar had explored the powers of terror. He had come to see fear of the unknown as one of the basic human emotions. He saw many different kinds of fear. People had fear of dark rooms, fear of the night, and fear of crazy people. He believed that, above all, humans felt a terrible, deep fear of death. He thought such fears could give him the material for fine poetry and endless story ideas. Horror of the unknown became a common theme in Edgar's works. He began to write about nervous, crazed characters who came face-to-face with death.

EDITOR FOR THE *MESSENGER*

Early next spring, Edgar learned that John Allan had died on March 27, 1834. It had been months since Edgar had written to his foster father. Allan left most of his fortune to his second wife. Edgar got nothing. Again, he felt he had been abandoned.

To try to lift his spirits, Edgar turned to John Pendleton Kennedy, an editor for the *Visiter*. Kennedy was keen to help get Edgar's tales published. Kennedy sent Edgar's tales to Carey, Lea, and Carey in Philadelphia. He sold one of Edgar's stories to a magazine for $15 (about $300). Kennedy also introduced Edgar to Thomas W. White. He owned the *Southern Literary Messenger*, a Richmond magazine. White asked Poe for essays, stories, and reviews. The *Messenger*, White explained, could use a skilled writer with some knowledge of literature. White agreed to publish several of Edgar's new stories, including "Berenice" and "Morella."

Thomas W. White

"Berenice" describes a quiet man, Egaeus, who spends much of his time daydreaming. He falls in love with his cousin, Berenice. He is fascinated by her teeth. After she becomes ill, Berenice is buried alive. Egaeus steals into her tomb at night, opens the coffin, and rips out her teeth. "Morella" is the tale of a man who can't forget his dead wife. He blurts out her name at the christening of his daughter. The mother's spirit is then reborn in the baby.

In the summer of 1835, White hired Edgar as an editor at $10 (about $200) a week. Edgar was happy to be earning a salary. He said good-bye to Maria and Virginia and moved back to Richmond. At the offices of the *Messenger*, he edited manuscripts and answered letters. In just a few months, the *Messenger* gained several thousand new readers. The readers liked Poe's writing. His sharp criticism of writers and their works became popular.

IN LOVE WITH VIRGINIA

After many years of struggle, Edgar was finally making money. He could buy decent clothes and eat well every day. Yet he still felt unhappy and lonely. He missed Virginia. He began drinking.

The *Southern Literary Messenger* was published in this building while Edgar was an editor there. The job provided Edgar with a steady income.

He drank so much that White threatened to fire him. Finally, White told Edgar that he could no longer work at the *Messenger* unless he stopped drinking forever.

Edgar tried. He knew that people depended on him. Maria Clemm was still very poor. He had been sending her money. His grandmother, Elizabeth Poe, had also passed on. Maria's son, Henry, had gone off to sea. Maria and Virginia were living alone together.

That summer, Neilson Poe, Edgar's cousin, invited Maria and Virginia into his household. Neilson made a good living. He offered to help Maria and to pay for Virginia's education.

When Edgar heard this news, he became deeply depressed. What would he do if Maria and Virginia left? He could not forget Virginia's large eyes and her delicate face. He could not let her go. He realized he was desperately in love with her. He wanted to marry her. He wrote a long, heartfelt letter to Maria. In it, he confessed that he loved Virginia with all his heart. He said he did not want to be parted from her.

Maria hesitated. Then she agreed not to part Virginia and Edgar. She felt close to him. He had taken care of her poor family as well as he could. She also knew that he saw her as a steady, guiding hand. She did not want to see him in despair. She decided not to move into Neilson Poe's home.

The next week, Edgar traveled to Baltimore. In September 1835, Edgar and Virginia signed a marriage license. Virginia was only thirteen years old. Few girls got married this young. Early the next month, Edgar brought the Clemm family to

Richmond. In the meantime, White had written to him. His letter urged Edgar to give up drinking. Good things would happen, White wrote, if he took better care of himself.

By the end of October 1835, Edgar had returned to the *Southern Literary Messenger*. On May 16, 1836, he married Virginia Clemm. The ceremony took place in the boardinghouse where they lived.

Edgar and his cousin Virginia were officially married in 1836. On the marriage license, Edgar listed Virginia's age as twenty-one. Edgar was twenty-seven.

People in Richmond criticized Edgar for marrying the thirteen-year-old Virginia. Edgar realized that Virginia was very young and still immature. But he was devoted to his young wife. She felt just as strongly about him. He vowed never to abandon her as his father had done his mother. But he had to get back to work.

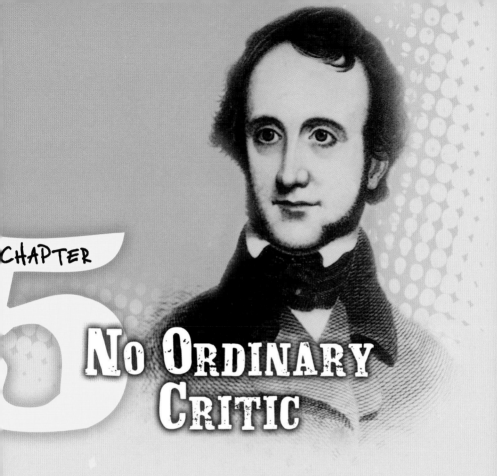

5

No Ordinary Critic

Edgar Allan Poe was no ordinary critic. He sometimes praised the writings he reviewed. But more often, he poked fun at them. He made fun of novelists, poets, and playwrights. He criticized faults in grammar.

In the *Messenger*, Edgar wrote reviews of anything that had been published. He wrote reviews of travel diaries and scientific papers. He was especially interested in poetry. In his articles,

After his marriage, Edgar (*above*) worked hard to make money for his wife and aunt.

he explained how poets should write. He described how their words could be powerful or beautiful or scary. Edgar's reviews even drew reviews of their own. In the *Cincinnati Mirror*, the editor wrote about the *Southern Literary Messenger*. One reviewer said that Edgar's reviews had "spice and spirit."

Some writers fought back with taunting letters and bad reviews of Edgar's own works. These wars of words sometimes lasted for weeks or months. Edgar enjoyed the fights. His editors enjoyed the interest he was stirring up. Rivalry among writers caught the public's notice.

Edgar was living as well as he ever had. His salary helped him provide a good life for Virginia, Maria, and himself. His health improved, and he stopped drinking. His family had enough to eat. He could buy himself new clothes. He made a good impression as he walked the familiar streets of Richmond.

New Stories

White not only paid Edgar a weekly salary. Edgar also earned extra money for short stories published in the *Messenger*. Edgar wrote mysteries and adventure stories. He even penned some comic tales.

The public's attention to Edgar's stories and reviews continued. But trouble was brewing at the *Southern Literary Messenger*. White was facing growing debts. The bitter reviews that Edgar wrote were beginning to draw criticism of the magazine itself. At the same time, Edgar felt that White did not give him enough credit for the magazine's success. He felt he should be earning more money. In January 1837, the *Messenger* announced that Edgar was leaving the magazine.

Edgar, Virginia, and Maria moved to New York. A bookseller named William Gowans had introduced Edgar to the city's important writers and editors. But 1837 was also a year of financial crisis for the United States. Many magazines and newspapers went out of business. So Edgar had no luck finding a job.

IT'S A FACT!

The financial crisis that rocked Edgar's world was called the Panic of 1837. The U.S. government had given extra tax money to the states. The states invested the money in local banks and businesses. The banks used the money to buy up land in the West, in the hope of selling it later for a big profit. This plan didn't work. Businesses and banks failed as a result.

Edgar's name as a writer was spreading. But no publishers had yet agreed to come out with his *Eleven Tales of the Arabesque*. Short stories didn't sell, the editors claimed. The market for books of any kind was small. People who did read wanted novels, not story collections.

Edgar didn't give up. He tried to find a style that would appeal to a wide audience. He looked around him for the works that were popular at the time. For example, he admired the stories of fantasy and horror that were fashionable in Germany. He also enjoyed *Robinson Crusoe*, the famous tale of a man lost at sea. He studied *The Rime of the Ancient Mariner*, a poem by Samuel Taylor Coleridge. He read *Mutiny on the Bounty*, the true account of a rebellion aboard a British ship.

These works inspired Edgar to create his longest work of fiction, *The Narrative of Arthur Gordon Pym*. For this work, Poe used the facts of a true-life Antarctic expedition by a man named Jeremiah Reynolds.

Edgar's story combined adventure with science. It describes Pym, a sailor from Nantucket, Massachusetts, who has a series of

Poe Walking High Bridge is a print inspired by Edgar and his works. He is shown as a lonely writer crossing an empty bridge in New York City. The print reflects the spooky feelings that Edgar presented in his poetry and short stories.

terrifying adventures at sea. Pym meets pirates, mutineers, and a ship full of corpses. Finally, he ends his voyage in the frozen seas of Antarctica.

Edgar was delighted when parts of the book were published in the *Messenger*. Soon afterward, in July 1838, the publisher Harper and Brothers came out with *The Narrative of Arthur Gordon Pym, of Nantucket.*

PHILADELPHIA

In the summer of 1838, Edgar moved his family again. This time, they went to Philadelphia. He still hoped to find the fame he felt he deserved. But jobs were hard to find in Philadelphia too. The next year, William Burton hired Edgar as the editor of *Burton's Gentleman's Magazine.*

Burton had started *Burton's* in 1837, but the magazine was already in trouble. Philadelphia had many magazines and newspapers. The competition for readers was fierce. And the costs for paper and printing were high. Burton was losing money. He offered Edgar only $10 a week. This was the same salary Edgar had earned at the *Southern Literary Messenger* two years earlier. Burton promised to raise Edgar's salary the next year if he

IT'S A FACT!

Burton's Gentleman's Magazine came out every month. It offered its readers articles on a wide variety of topics. These topics ranged from general-interest news to poetry and stories. Edgar published a number of stories in *Burton's* while he worked there as an editor.

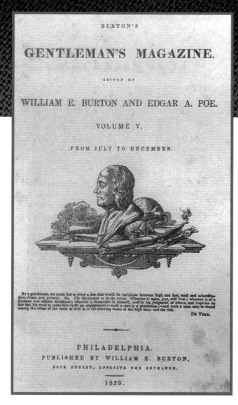

stayed with the magazine. Edgar would need to spend only two hours a day at the magazine's offices. In June 1839, the two men came to an agreement. Burton hired thirty-year-old Edgar as an assistant editor.

CHAPTER 6

FIRST PUBLICATIONS

Edgar *(above)* **enjoyed working for William Burton.**

FOR EDGAR, BURTON PROVED TO BE a wonderful person to work for. He was also a more interesting man than William White. Burton was an experienced comic actor. He had played clowns and drunks on the stages of the United States and Great Britain. Burton thought of himself a British gentleman. Yet, he was always getting into trouble. The gossips of Philadelphia loved to spread rumors about him. Unfortunately, the rumors often turned out to be true.

Burton didn't mind his fame. He believed it might help him achieve his two ambitions. One goal was to run a theater of his own. The other ambition was to publish the most popular magazine in the United States.

In the summer of 1839, Edgar wrote nearly every review that appeared in *Burton's*. His reputation as a severe critic worried his new boss. But Burton also knew he could count on Edgar for good writing.

Edgar moved his family into a nice home. After being at the office, he went home and worked hard at his writing. He often worked late into the night, writing and revising. He took care of his wife and his aunt. He kept away from strong drink. He also had friends and coworkers to dinner.

A First Mystery

This happier life didn't change Edgar's writing. His stories were still dark and terrifying. "The Fall of the House of Usher" was printed in the September 1839 issue of *Burton's*. This gloomy tale is told by a young man whose name is never mentioned. The narrator arrives at the home of an old friend,

Roderick Usher, whom he has not seen in many years. Usher lives in a broken-down house with his twin sister, Madeline. From his first sight of the House of Usher, a strange dread overcomes the narrator:

> I looked upon the scene before me—upon the mere house, and the simple landscape features of the domain—upon the bleak walls—upon the vacant eye-like windows— upon a few rank sedges—and upon a few white trunks of decayed trees—with an utter depression of soul. . . . There was an iciness, a sinking, a sickening of the heart— an unredeemed dreariness.

The House of Usher is slowly crumbling into the swamp that surrounds it. Usher himself looks like a corpse. His deep-set, glowing eyes give him a terrifying expression.

Madeline dies of a strange disease. Her body is put into a coffin. The narrator and Usher bury her coffin in a tomblike room underneath the house. Then, one stormy night, a strange sound is heard from the underground tomb. Madeline appears at

This illustration of Roderick and Madeline Usher appeared in a printing of "The Fall of the House of Usher."

the door of the room. She has clawed her way out of the coffin where she has been buried alive. She flails about, struggling for breath, and kills her brother. The narrator runs away from the House of Usher. He watches the house collapse with a loud noise, like a clap of thunder.

After "The Fall of the House of Usher," more of Edgar's tales appeared in *Burton's*. Edgar's name was spreading among the general public. Lea and Blanchard published a complete edition of his stories under the name *Tales of the Grotesque and*

Arabesque. Edgar received no actual money. Lea and Blanchard kept all the profits. But the company gave Poe the right to republish the stories in a book or a magazine.

Between his job and his writing, Edgar was still earning very little money. He worked hard to improve his stories. He had one goal–to be a well-known writer. He was certain he had loads of talent. He was bitter about the failure of the world to see him as he saw himself.

IT'S A FACT!

Respected book reviewers praised *Tales of the Grotesque and Arabesque.* However, Edgar—like other authors of his time—took no chances. He wrote glowing but anonymous reviews of his own work. He'd publish them in one magazine to promote his stories that had appeared in another magazine.

WASTED TALENTS

With Burton's permission, Edgar also contributed to other magazines. In January 1840, he challenged the readers of *Alexander's Weekly Messenger* to send him a cipher (code) that he could not solve. To make the ciphers, readers were to replace each letter of a phrase with a different letter. Hundreds of readers took up Edgar's challenge and sent in their ciphers. Edgar solved them all. His cipher articles drew more public attention to his talents. He began to see himself not only as a writer and critic but also as a deep thinker. He was a man with a talent for solving problems of all kinds.

Edgar began to think that he was wasting his talent at *Burton's*. The steady weekly salary and freelance writing were bringing in enough money to provide for his household. But he spent most of his time answering letters from readers. The magazine bored and sometimes annoyed him. Many of its articles seemed silly or gossipy.

An answer to his problems had already occurred to the young author. He would start a magazine of his own. He would call it the *Penn*. When Burton heard about

IT'S A FACT!

When he chose the *Penn* as his magazine's name, Edgar was playing on the name of the family that founded Pennsylvania. He was living in Pennsylvania at the time. The word *pen* comes from the old Latin word for "feather." It may be a reference to the feathered quill used as a writing tool in Edgar's time.

Edgar's plans, he and Edgar argued. Burton accused Edgar of planning to steal readers from *Burton's*.

During the argument, Edgar had bad things to say too. Burton had left all the editorial work up to Edgar. Burton had unfairly rejected articles Edgar had written. Edgar heard that Burton was planning to sell the magazine without telling him.

After another argument, Edgar left *Burton's*. Soon afterward, Burton gave up on the magazine business. In November 1840, he sold *Burton's* to George Rex Graham, who renamed it *Graham's Magazine*.

Edgar began planning the *Penn*. He decided it would be a national magazine. Writers from all over the country—not just from Boston or New York—would write for it. Instead of gossip, Edgar wanted the *Penn* to present "fearless and honest opinion." The opinions would be about writers and their writing. The *Penn* wouldn't bother with politics, society news, or travel stories.

In the summer of 1840, Edgar wrote a business plan. It described the magazine for the investors he was hoping to attract. Certain of his coming success, Edgar listed five hundred possible subscribers. These people would subscribe to (buy) the magazine every month. Writers and editors had suggested the potential subscribers. The first issue of the *Penn* was to appear in 1841. But in January 1841, the United States had another financial crisis.

Businesses shut down. Many banks closed. Paper money lost its value. Few people had money to spend on a magazine subscription. Edgar put off publishing the first issue of the *Penn* from January to March 1841. Then he dropped his plans altogether.

A NEW FASHION

Edgar still didn't give up on his goal. He began writing for George Rex Graham. In April 1841, *Graham's Magazine* printed "The Murders in the Rue Morgue." The tale is set in Paris, France. It features a skillful amateur (not professional) detective, C. Auguste Dupin. He isn't part of the police force. But the Paris police ask Dupin to help them solve a puzzling murder.

George Rex Graham

The crime has taken place inside a locked room. Dupin carefully examines the room, the doors, the windows, and the fireplace. He looks at the courtyard outside the room. He thinks through all the possibilities. He finally uncovers the murderer by using simple logic.

In "The Murders in the Rue Morgue," Edgar created an entirely new character—the amateur detective. This character uncovers clues and solves crimes that have stumped the police. The popularity of Edgar's story pointed out a change in U.S. society. The country was growing quickly. More people than ever before were living in large cities. Newspapers and magazines in these cities described terrible crimes. Mystery stories became hugely popular. The most popular stories had violent plots and tricky puzzles for readers to solve.

IT'S A FACT!

The traits that made Auguste Dupin a great detective—attention to detail, analysis, and intuition—inspired later authors of detective fiction. Mystery fans still love to read stories where Sherlock Holmes or Miss Marple outwit the police and solve the case.

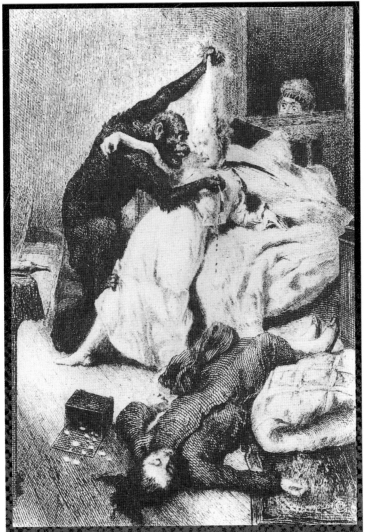

The title illustration for "The Murders in the Rue Morgue" shows an apelike monster attacking a woman while another woman watches. A murdered woman lies on the floor.

To *Graham's* readers, "The Murders in the Rue Morgue" was more appealing than the best poetry. People bought up the magazine as soon as it was published. In just a few months, Edgar's other articles and tales helped *Graham's* increase its circulation from 3,500 to 37,000. As Edgar's fame spread, *Graham's* became a hugely popular monthly magazine.

AN UNHAPPY NIGHT

One night in 1842, Edgar sat down with guests in his warm and comfortable house. The company enjoyed a hearty meal. Then they gathered by the fireplace to hear Virginia sing.

Edgar felt satisfied with his life. He loved his nineteen-year-old wife and enjoyed living with Maria. He was sure he would write more successful stories and win an even larger audience. He saw higher salaries in his future. Soon his name would be known all over the world.

Suddenly, the music stopped. Virginia lost her voice in a fit of violent coughing. Edgar leaped forward. He gathered his wife in his arms and carried her to bed. He covered her with a coat and summoned a doctor.

The doctor examined Virginia. He told Edgar and Maria that Virginia had tuberculosis. This was the same slow and fatal lung disease that had killed his mother, Eliza Poe. Virginia grew weaker but didn't die. Edgar fell into helpless despair as he watched his wife's health get worse.

CHAPTER 7

LITERARY SUCCESSES

AFTER LEARNING of Virginia's illness, Edgar became hard to work with. He still felt the world didn't recognize his writing talent. He also felt Graham wasn't paying him what he was worth. Edgar knew Graham was making a profit on his magazine. Graham was underpaying his staff. He was also not rewarding Edgar, who was doing the most to help the magazine succeed.

Edgar also grew more sensitive to criticism. He got into loud arguments with Charles Peterson, another editor at *Graham's*. These fights ended Edgar's days at *Graham's*. One day in April 1842, Edgar arrived to find another editor sitting at his desk, using all his writing supplies. Edgar turned toward the door and left the offices of *Graham's* for good.

Edgar knew better things were in store for him. He thought he might soon be published in Great Britain. Just before he left *Graham's*, he had met Charles Dickens. This famous British author was touring the United States. Edgar spoke with Dickens and gave him a copy of *Tales of the Grotesque and Arabesque*. He asked Dickens to find a British publisher for the *Tales*. Dickens promised to try.

Meanwhile, Edgar brought back Monsieur Dupin in another detective story. He based the new story, "The Mystery of Marie Rogêt," on the real murder of Mary Cecilia Rogers. The actual murder had taken place in New York. Edgar changed the name of the victim and moved the story to Paris.

IT'S A FACT!

Edgar wasn't afraid to critique the work of literary greats, including Charles Dickens. Poe generally praised the British writer's work, but he also pointed out some flaws. He warned his readers not to assume a book was good simply because a famous author had written it.

STRANGE BEHAVIOR

In June 1842, Edgar left his family at home in Philadelphia. He was traveling to New York to search for a job. He was also trying to sell his works to other publishers. New York was a bustling literary world. Poets and magazine editors met to discuss the latest writing. Fitz-Greene Halleck, one of the city's best-known authors, wrote funny stories about life in New York. Evert Duyckinck edited the *Literary World.* He held a gathering for writers at his home.

Upon arriving in the city, Edgar accepted an invitation to stay with friends. In the evenings, he talked, ate, and laughed with his companions. But he also drank and lost control of himself. He walked the streets, acting strangely. He talked to the buildings and the sidewalks. Another time, Edgar behaved badly in the offices of editors and publishers he was trying to impress. This string of scenes lasted for days. On another occasion, he crossed the Hudson River by ferry and wandered through the woods of northern New Jersey. A search party found him shouting. He seemed to be unsure of where he was.

A Theory about Poe's Behavior

Edgar's behavior later in his life was certainly odd. One theory suggests he had a lesion (abnormal area) in his brain. Results of such a problem might include an unsteady heartbeat and an unusual reaction to alcohol. Because of the lesion, any liquor Edgar drank could bring on a kind of insanity. This matches what others saw when Poe had even one drink.

When he returned to Philadelphia, Edgar found himself no closer to his goals. Another economic panic in the United States was ruining many banks and businesses. Nobody had any money to invest in the magazine he still hoped to start. Desperate, Edgar finally decided to declare himself bankrupt.

In the fall of 1842, Edgar decided to try to get a different kind of job. He wanted one that would pay better than writing. He would find work as a clerk for the U.S. government. The job would be easy, he thought, and would leave him time to write. The new U.S. president was John Tyler. Edgar believed Tyler might appoint him as a clerk in the Philadelphia Customs House.

To get the job, Edgar wrote a letter to Frederick W. Thomas, a friend and clerk in the Treasury Department. Thomas was also a friend of Robert Tyler, the president's son. Thomas encouraged Edgar's hopes. From Washington, Thomas reported that the government might help Edgar start his own magazine if the publication would support the goals of the new president.

In September 1842, Edgar went to Washington, D.C. He was to meet with Thomas and important people in the Tyler administration. But again Edgar seemed to become his own worst enemy. He began to drink and to act strangely. He came down with chills and a fever. He rambled through the streets. He wore his mud-spattered coat turned inside out. He didn't show up for his meeting with Frederick Thomas. Three weeks later, he went to the Philadelphia Customs House to ask about his appointment. An official told him there would be no more appointments.

SCREAMS IN THE NIGHT

Edgar kept writing. In January 1843, the *Pioneer* magazine of Boston published a new tale by Edgar, "The Tell-Tale Heart." The story began:

True!—nervous—very, very dreadfully
nervous I had been and am; but why will
you say that I am mad? The disease had
sharpened my senses—not destroyed—not
dulled them. Above all was the sense of
hearing. . . . I heard all things in the
heaven and in the earth. I heard many
things in hell. How, then, am I mad?
Hearken! and observe how healthily—how
calmly I can tell you the whole story.

An illustration from a version of "The Tell-Tale Heart"

The narrator murders an old man in his bed and cuts apart the corpse. He hides the body parts beneath the floorboards of the room. He believes nobody will be able to find out about the evil deed. The secret is safe.

Neighbors reported hearing a scream coming from the house in the middle of the night. Police detectives arrive to investigate. They begin asking questions. Suddenly, a low, dull, quick sound begins to rise from beneath the floor. The narrator gasps for breath. But the police seem to hear nothing. Finally, the murderer can't stand it:

Villains! . . . I admit the deed!—tear up the planks! here, here!—it is the beating of his hideous heart!

It's a Fact!

Check out the Further Reading section on page 109 for a list of websites where you can read Poe's works.

The ghoulish "Tell-Tale Heart" thrilled and terrified Edgar's readers. Such a story made the public curious about its author. Edgar must be quite strange, they thought. Perhaps he was even evil. What must he be hiding behind his carefully chosen words? What strange sounds must be echoing in his head?

"THE GOLD BUG" AND "THE PIT"

Edgar renamed his hoped-for magazine the *Stylus*. Thomas C. Clarke, a wealthy Philadelphia publisher, agreed to help him publish it. In the meantime, Edgar finished "The Gold Bug." The story describes a mysterious treasure hunt on a South Carolina island. Edgar wanted to print the story in the first issue of the *Stylus*, but he didn't have the money. When the *Dollar Newspaper* announced a short-story contest that would award $100 for first place, Edgar sent in "The Gold Bug." It won the prize and appeared on June 28, 1843.

IT'S A FACT!

Edgar changed the name of his magazine to the *Stylus*. *Stylus* is another word for "a writing tool."

"The Gold Bug" covered the entire front page of the newspaper. The story made thirty-four-year-old Edgar famous throughout the United States. In response to this first best-seller, Graham agreed to publish a new edition of Poe's works, named *The*

This is the living room of Edgar's home in Philadelphia. He lived in the house in 1843 and 1844. The home has been fully restored.

Prose Romances of Edgar A. Poe. It was to be the first in a series of books. The first edition appeared later in 1843. It included "The Murders in the Rue Morgue" and "The Man That Was Used Up."

Edgar and Graham had made plans to print more editions. But only the one edition of *The Prose Romances of Edgar A. Poe* came out. Story collections were still not selling well. Readers continued to like stories that appeared only in magazines. Such stories were brief entertainment. People enjoyed them in the evening while sitting by the fire.

In the fall of 1843, Edgar published another gruesome story. It was called "The Pit and the Pendulum." The nightmarish tale describes a prisoner trapped in a pitch-black dungeon. He stumbles along the walls. He is desperately trying to understand the size and shape of his cell. He falls unconscious. He awakes to find himself strapped to a slab of stone. A sharp blade is swinging above him. It is slowly descending. As the blade slices at his clothing, hungry rats swarm around him. The prisoner makes a last effort to save himself.

"THE RAVEN"

Edgar's mystery stories were catching on with the public. But he still thought of himself as a poet. For him, composing good poetry was the greatest challenge for any writer. In late 1843, he began to work on a new poem.

Edgar divided the poem into seventeen stanzas (divisions). He carefully put together the lines of each stanza. He paid attention to each stanza's words and rhythm. He wanted the reader to sense his feelings of sadness, fear, and regret. For weeks, he struggled to describe what he was seeing in his head. He saw a dark room and a black bird that sings a single, mysterious word. Edgar wanted readers to feel the narrator's bitter memories of a long-lost love. He began to read the first stanza of the poem to the entire staff of *Graham's.*

> Once upon a midnight dreary, while I
>   pondered, weak and weary,
> Over many a quaint and curious volume of
>   forgotten lore–
> While I nodded, nearly napping, suddenly
>   there came a tapping,
> As of some one gently rapping, rapping at
>   my chamber door.
> "Tis some visitor," I muttered, "tapping at
>   my chamber door;
> Only this and nothing more."

The narrator of the poem spends many hours trying to forget a woman named Lenore, whom he has lost forever. He's sitting in a dark room and is reading to distract himself from his sorrow. All the while, he hears a tapping sound. Finally, to discover where the tapping is coming from, he

flings open a window. A
black raven flies into the
room. The bird perches on
a marble statue of Pallas, a
figure from Greek
mythology. The bird can
speak only one word:
"Nevermore!"

IT'S A FACT!

Pallas was the Greek
goddess of wisdom
and warfare. She was
sometimes also
called Pallas Athena.

The air in the room grows thick. The narrator
screams angrily at the bird. He demands to know
why the bird has invaded his room. What does it
mean by croaking the same word over and over?
Here's the last stanza:

And the Raven, never flitting, still is sitting,
   still is sitting.
On the pallid bust of Pallas just above my
   chamber door;
And his eyes have all the seeming of a
   demon's that is dreaming,
And the lamplight o'er him streaming throws
   his shadow on the floor;
And my soul from out that shadow that lies
   floating on the floor
Shall be lifted–nevermore!

After Edgar finished reading, the men at *Graham's* muttered their disappointment. They pitied Edgar for writing such a silly poem. The magazine would not publish it. But the editors "passed the hat" for the author. They collected $15 and gave the money to Edgar. Humiliated, Edgar accepted the money. He left the office, still holding the rejected "Raven" in his hands.

Edgar decided to leave Philadelphia for good. His own magazine, the *Stylus*, had yet to come out. He and Virginia returned to

IT'S A FACT!

Edgar is the first writer to be honored by professional football. In 1996, the city of Baltimore was adding a team to the National Football League. The team chose the name the Baltimore Ravens, after the most famous poem of the city's former resident.

New York. They lived in a boardinghouse, where the two received a warm welcome from the owners. (Maria Clemm would come as soon as they were settled.) That night, Mr. and Mrs. Poe ate well, better than they had in many weeks.

Edgar's goal was to make his fortune in New York. He thought the city was bigger, richer, and perhaps more understanding of his talent than Philadelphia. He planned to sell his works to New York magazines. In this busy city, everyone seemed to have a business or was starting one. Here, he would raise enough money to begin his own magazine.

CHAPTER 8

A SERIES OF SETBACKS

Edgar may have drawn this self-portrait. He was in his mid-thirties.

AT FIRST, NEW YORK GAVE Edgar no better job chances than Philadelphia did. Edgar fell ill and spent many days lying in bed. Virginia's illness often stopped her from leaving the house. Maria came to the rescue. She walked through the large city. She called on editors and publishers, trying to help her son-in-law. In the fall of 1844, she went to see Nathaniel Willis, the editor of the *New York Evening Mirror*. Willis agreed to hire Edgar at a salary of $15 a week.

Edgar wrote hundreds of short "fillers" for the *Mirror*. Most of these articles gossiped about famous writers or actors. Edgar didn't mind gossiping about famous people. But he quickly grew bored with writing about them. Most of the fillers didn't even name the author. His work for the *Mirror* did nothing to make Edgar known to the public or the critics.

But on January 29, 1845, the *Mirror* printed the poem that would make thirty-six-year-old Edgar one of the most famous writers in the country. "The Raven" appeared in a single long column on the *Mirror*'s back page.

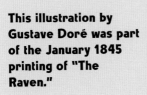

This illustration by Gustave Doré was part of the January 1845 printing of "The Raven."

Soon afterward, newspapers in other large U.S. cities reprinted the poem. "The Raven" became a huge success.

MOVING TO THE *BROADWAY JOURNAL*

The popularity of "The Raven" made Edgar believe his writings would make a success of any magazine he joined. His confidence pushed him to make an agreement with the owners of the *Broadway Journal.* They would pay him one-third of the magazine's profits instead of a weekly salary. In exchange, he would provide at least one page of material for each new issue.

Edgar moved from the offices of the *Mirror* to those of the *Journal.* To supply his weekly material, he reprinted many of his tales and poems. He wrote reviews of books and plays. He commented on the literary scene. He worked hard, often staying at his desk well into the evening. He hoped to turn the fame he had won with "The Raven" and "The Gold Bug" into fortune.

Despite his hard work, Edgar found himself earning one-third of almost nothing. The *Journal* barely made a profit. Through the summer of 1845, his frustration grew worse. Edgar came to think it

was almost impossible for a writer to make a living.
The public still saw books as a luxury. Few
bookstores existed, even in large cities. Even fewer
sold collections of poems or short stories. And
newspapers and magazines paid little money to the
people who wrote for them.

Edgar began drinking again and going on
aimless walks. This behavior angered his friends.
He couldn't stand to see other writers—such as
Henry Longfellow and Ralph Waldo Emerson—

**Edgar was frustrated with the fame achieved by writers Henry
Wadsworth Longfellow *(left)* and Ralph Waldo Emerson *(right)*.**

earn more praise and money than he did. He watched the fame he had earned with "The Raven" slip away. He got more angry with his own poverty. He saw others being mean to him at every turn. He imagined his rivals plotting his destruction. He felt alone again, as he had felt when he was a boy. Once again, the world grew dark and threatening.

TRANSCENDENTALISM

When Edgar was alive, the best-known U.S. writers lived in New England—particularly in and near Boston, Massachusetts. These writers included Ralph Waldo Emerson and Henry David Thoreau. Both men belonged to a movement called Transcendentalism. This movement was a reaction to the strict teachings of a Protestant faith called Calvinism. This faith taught that people were naturally sinful and must be saved. Transcendentalists believed that human beings could discover truth without a church. All they needed was a pure spirit that transcended (rose above) day-to-day worries and habits.

Edgar, however, didn't belong to the movement. In fact, he thought New Englanders were snobby and self-satisfied. These northerners would never welcome him, a humble man from the South. He did not share the movement's social concerns either. These concerns included temperance (avoiding liquor), woman's rights, and ending slavery. Edgar's goal was to trigger strong feelings of fear or the love of beauty in his readers. He wasn't interested in leading them to a better life.

A RETURN TO BOSTON

Edgar knew there was more than one way to earn a living by writing. Many people in U.S. cities enjoyed going to evening lectures. Writers, editors, politicians, and European visitors appeared in public halls. They would give speeches on nearly any topic. They earned a percentage of the money taken in by the ticket sales.

That fall, Edgar gave a lecture in Boston. Even though he had been born there, Edgar saw the city as enemy territory. Boston was the home of some of the nation's best-known writers and critics. But Edgar thought most of them were snobs. Boston was hostile to Edgar's childhood home state of Virginia. Boston's people

IT'S A FACT!

In the 1800s, authors, explorers, and adventurers often found quick money by going on a lecture tour. In each city they visited, they would rent a hall and create ads for their talk. As payment, they'd receive part of the ticket sales. Mark Twain, for example, made a lot of money this way. Edgar wasn't so successful.

strongly disapproved of slavery, which was still legal in Virginia.

Edgar announced that he would write a new poem for the appearance. He said it would be as good as "The Raven." But try as he might, he found no inspiration to write the new poem. On the evening of October 16, he arrived in Boston. That night, he gave a long and dreary performance. Instead of delivering a new poem, he recited "Al Aaraaf," a work he had written almost twenty years earlier. Edgar recited the poem's 260 lines in front of an impatient audience. He seemed to almost want to anger them. Most of the audience walked out of the hall before he finally recited "The Raven."

A MAGAZINE OF HIS OWN

By the fall of 1845, Charles Briggs, co-owner of the *Broadway Journal*, was tired of Edgar's drinking. Briggs wanted to get out of the magazine business. He allowed Edgar and John Bisco, another *Journal* editor, to buy his share of the magazine. Bisco and Edgar then became partners.

Edgar saw this move as his chance to finally run a magazine of his own. But the *Journal* was in

financial trouble. The magazine owed money to a
lot of printers. Not much money was in the
magazine's bank account. Bisco decided to give up
his share of the partnership. Edgar suddenly
became the sole owner of the *Broadway Journal.* He
wrote to old friends and even to some old enemies.
He begged for money to help him keep the
magazine going. Horace Greeley, editor of the *New
York Tribune,* agreed to loan him $50. But that
wasn't enough to pay for everything. He begged for
money from others.

In spite of these efforts, Edgar could not find
the money to pay his writers. He found himself
overwhelmed with all the tasks of publishing the
Journal. Because he was too busy to write new
material, he simply reprinted old poems and tales.
By the end of the year, he realized the magazine
was failing. He signed over half-ownership of the
Journal to Thomas Lane, a friend from Philadelphia.
On January 3, Lane decided to close down the
Journal for good.

A TALE OF REVENGE

In May 1846, Edgar again escaped from New York.
He moved Maria and frail twenty-three-year-old

Virginia to the fresh air of the countryside. The family rented a small farm in Fordham, a town north of New York City. In the same month, Edgar began writing a column for *Godey's* magazine in Philadelphia. He passed along gossip about New York literary figures.

Edgar also made some enemies with his gossip columns. Among them was Thomas Dunn English, a poet from Philadelphia. They carried on a mean literary fight. English spread rumors about Edgar's character. He accused him of copying his works from others. When Edgar proved that the charge

Edgar, Virginia, and Maria moved into this cottage outside New York City in 1846.

was false, English repeated it. He dared Edgar to sue him. Edgar did in July 1846. Eventually, Edgar won the lawsuit. He collected a small sum for damage done to his reputation.

In the fall of 1846, he finished a new story, "The Cask of Amontillado." The topic was the desire for revenge. The narrator is Montresor. He lures his enemy, named Fortunato, to a cellar. He's promised Fortunato a taste of the finest Amontillado wine. Fortunato agrees to come. In the cellar, Montresor chains Fortunato to a wall. He begins laying a brick wall. It will seal Fortunato into a tomb. His enemy will die of hunger, thirst, and fear.

A DEATH AT HOME

"The Cask of Amontillado" appeared in November 1846, in *Godey's* magazine. But soon Edgar would have another horrible reason to feel sad and bitter. Winter was coming. The cold, damp weather was making Virginia worse. She was dying. Edgar could not even afford to give her a comfortable bed. Virginia slept on a bed of straw, covered with the old military coat Edgar had worn at West Point.

Friends collected some money so Edgar could give his wife a more comfortable bed. On December

15, 1846, the *New York Express* published a plea for
help for the Poes. Some admirers passed money to
Edgar without giving their
names. But no amount of
money could cure
Virginia's illness. There was
nothing any doctor could
do. Edgar and Maria
watched helplessly as
Virginia slipped away on
January 30, 1847.

IT'S A FACT!

Virginia was twenty-four when she died of tuberculosis. She died at the same age and of the same illness as Poe's mother and brother.

On January 31, Edgar
placed his wife's open coffin on his writing table for
viewing, as was customary at that time. Neighbors
arrived to pay their last respects. A small
procession began outside. Edgar buried his wife in
the graveyard of the Fordham Dutch Reformed
Church.

Virginia's death turned Edgar into a silent,
mourning shadow. He wandered through the house
like a ghost. In the worst moments of grief, he
drowned his sorrows with drink.

CHAPTER 9

FINAL JOURNEYS

AFTER VIRGINIA'S DEATH, Edgar spent most of his time at the Fordham cottage he and Maria shared. He felt too depressed to leave the house. His troubled mind stopped him from working. He wasn't sleeping much either. To ease his depression, he took nighttime walks to Virginia's nearby tomb. He would sit there for hours, not moving or speaking.

To help Edgar, Nathaniel Willis printed Edgar's poems and reviews in the *Mirror*. Meanwhile, Maria again went to New York City, calling on friends and editors. She collected money for the household by begging. She also sold letters Edgar had received from famous writers.

"EUREKA"

Edgar slowly recovered from the loss of Virginia. In the summer of 1847, he began planning a triumphant return to New York City. He worked on an essay. He planned to read it at a lecture in New York to raise money for the *Stylus*.

Within months, Edgar was finishing his essay. He called it "Eureka." In this work, Edgar tried to explain the secrets of the solar system. Edgar intended "Eureka" to be a work of science and deep thinking. He would reveal the divine plan that had created the universe. But instead of equations or measurements, Edgar used his own thoughts and poetic inspiration.

IT'S A FACT!

In Greek, the word *eureka* means "I have found it." Maybe Edgar thought he'd found some of the secrets of the universe.

In its poetic way, "Eureka" predicted two important theories of modern physics. One was the big bang. This theory says the entire universe was created from a powerful explosion billions of years ago. The other theory was the big crunch. This theory says that, over time, the universe will shrink back to a single point.

But Edgar's lecture and reading of "Eureka" was a failure. On the night he was to give the reading, a fierce winter storm hit New York. Only sixty people fought their way through the ice and snow to come to the lecture. Edgar hardly made a cent. Few people could understand "Eureka." They felt Edgar was mocking their intelligence with his strange ideas.

AN ADMIRING RAVEN

People in the United States and Europe still enjoyed Edgar's tales and poems. Many readers sent him fan mail. Among them were many female admirers. They thought Edgar was handsome. And his scary stories and tragic life fascinated them. Edgar returned their attention. He felt lonely after Virginia's death, and he enjoyed the company of women.

In February 1848, Edgar received a poem from one of these female admirers. The sender had titled her work "To Edgar A. Poe." The writer tried to write in Edgar's own style in "The Raven." She even borrowed some of its phrases and rhymes. Edgar soon found out the poet's name and address.

It's a Fact!

Many writings about Edgar during his lifetime described him as handsome. He was said to have a broad forehead and a well-shaped head. Phrenology is the study of a person's character based on the shape of the skull. This was a popular science in Edgar's lifetime. Poe's large forehead was thought to show his intelligence.

He answered her with a poem of his own, calling it "To Helen."

Edgar remembered first seeing Sarah Helen Whitman in 1845, while he was in Providence, Rhode Island. Sarah wrote and published poetry. Many critics liked her work. After receiving her poem and writing his response, Edgar planned to see her again.

In September 1848, he left New York for Providence. He arrived at Sarah's front door. He spoke with her, quickly fell in love, and proposed marriage. Sarah's mother and the rest of her family disapproved of Edgar. Sarah sent him away. But she said she'd consider his proposal.

After Edgar left Providence, many of Sarah's friends began talking about him behind his back.

Edgar hoped to marry poet and admirer Sarah Helen Whitman (right).

They warned her that Edgar was untrustworthy. He was poor. He had many enemies. They said the true reason for his proposal wasn't love but greed. They said the Whitman family money, which Sarah would inherit, was the real attraction.

In early November, Edgar returned to Providence. He was ill and feverish. After seeing him this way, Sarah's mother and sister firmly set themselves against the marriage. But Sarah agreed to marry Edgar as long as he promised to stop drinking. Edgar made the promise. But his words didn't satisfy Sarah's angry mother. She threatened to cut Sarah out of her will if the marriage took place.

Edgar had this photograph taken in 1848 for Sarah Helen Whitman.

Edgar still pressed Sarah to marry him. He went back to Providence on December 20, 1848. Once again, he asked Sarah to marry him. But another anonymous attack on Edgar came in the form of a letter. The letter accused Edgar of breaking his promise not to drink. Sarah still loved Edgar. But she was uneasy. She decided not to go through with the marriage. Edgar, at thirty-nine, left Providence a very disappointed man.

TALE OF A JESTER

In the meantime, Edgar had been working on another tale of revenge, entitled "Hop-Frog." The story takes place in the castle of a cruel king. The king loves to make jokes at the expense of others. He especially picks on his jester (court clown), a crippled dwarf named Hop-Frog. One evening, the king forces Hop-Frog to drink wine, a beverage the jester can't stand.

Later, the king commands Hop-Frog to plan a costume party. The jester agrees and plans his revenge. He asks the king and seven of the king's ministers to dress as orangutans (a type of ape). He tells them that they will play a joke on the other guests. Hop-Frog chains the eight men together and covers their costumes with tar and straw. As the party gets noisier, the orangutans enter the hall. Their arrival causes a huge stir. They gather in the center of the room, gesturing wildly. Their screaming scatters the guests around the room. The king and his ministers enjoy the great joke.

Suddenly, Hop-Frog pulls the eight men up by the chains that bind them. They are hanging from the ceiling. He sets them on fire with a burning torch. The king and his ministers are burned alive in their costumes. The guests watch as the men die horrible deaths.

AN IDEA FROM THE WEST

In December 1848, a Boston magazine called the *Flag of Our Union* published "Hop-Frog." That same month, Edgar received a letter from E. H. N. Patterson. He lived in the small town of Oquawka, Illinois. Patterson wanted to start a literary journal. He wanted Edgar to be his editor. Edgar wrote back, telling Patterson the many ideas he had collected for the *Stylus*. He told Patterson he could gather twenty thousand subscribers. Edgar also asked Patterson for a loan of $50. He wanted to make a lecture tour through the South. He would give speeches to raise interest in the new journal.

Edgar was open to working with Patterson. But he believed that Oquawka was no place to publish

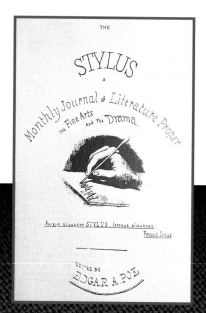

a literary magazine. He asked Patterson to move his office to Saint Louis, Missouri, about 200 miles (322 kilometers) to the south. Edgar wanted the new magazine to appeal to

This handmade copy of the *Stylus* was used to interest investors. But the magazine never got off the ground.

southern and western readers. The magazine would feature poets, essayists, and storytellers who were not from New York or Boston. Edgar wanted to shun these traditional centers of American writing.

Edgar still felt alone in the northeastern United States. He had never been part of the closely knit group of writers and editors who dominated the country's literature. He also didn't fit into New York's money-hungry society. Edgar still saw himself as a southerner. For him, a southerner put honor, good manners, and style above the desire for money. He saw himself as a stranger in these cold northeastern cities.

NORTH VS. SOUTH

Edgar was born in Boston, a city in the North. But he called himself a southerner because of his ties to the southern state of Virginia. During his lifetime, tensions were growing between the North and the South. The North, which made money from factories run by machinery, wanted to end slavery. Northerners thought slavery was wrong. In the South, farming was the main way to make money. Southerners wanted to keep slavery because the unpaid workers made their farms more profitable. As Americans took over lands in the West, more states were added to the United States. Should these new states allow slavery or forbid it? Should each state make its own rules, or should all states follow the same rules? Disagreement on these questions finally led to the Civil War (1861–1865).

GOING BACK TO RICHMOND

Virginia's death and Sarah Whitman's rejection still bothered Edgar. He felt like a failure in his personal and professional life. He began to lose his fear of death. He thought of death as a release from his suffering.

In early July 1849, Edgar was on his way to Richmond to begin a lecture tour. He stopped in Philadelphia, where he went on another drinking spree. He grew violently ill and started hearing voices. He was sure that a group of men was trying to kill him. The police arrested Edgar for drunkenness. After his release, he returned to the Philadelphia train depot to claim his suitcase. It held his belongings and his

Sarah Royster Shelton

lecture notes. To his dismay, the lecture notes had been stolen.

Finally, Edgar reached Richmond, where he moved into a hotel. He made a solemn vow to stop drinking for good. He also called on Sarah Royster. She was the girl he had written to from the University of Virginia twenty

years earlier. Sarah was now a wealthy widow named
Mrs. Shelton. But she had not forgotten the love she
had felt for Poe as a girl. She and Edgar renewed
their friendship. The two began planning to marry.

Edgar delivered successful lectures in Richmond
and Norfolk, Virginia. On September 27, 1849, he
boarded a steamer at the Richmond harbor. He
planned to stop in Baltimore, then continue on to
New York. He would pick up Maria Clemm from the
sad house in Fordham. He would pack his things,
close up the house, and return to Richmond. After all
the sadness and misfortune, he would return to old
friends. He would find a loyal audience for his works
and his lectures. He would enjoy a second chance
with an almost-forgotten love.

A MYSTERIOUS ENDING

On September 28, 1849, Edgar Allan Poe arrived in
Baltimore. It was rainy and cold in the city. Edgar
already felt very ill. In a hurry to complete his trip to
New York, he caught a train for Philadelphia. There,
he stayed at the home of an old friend named James
P. Moss. Edgar was feverish, and he rested before
moving on. When he felt well enough to travel again,
Edgar returned to the Philadelphia train station. But

instead of catching the train to New York, he
mistakenly boarded a train headed back to Baltimore.

Wednesday, October 3, was Election Day in
Baltimore. Voters were at the polls. Just outside one
of the polls, Poe ran into Joseph Walker, who
worked for the *Baltimore Sun*. Walker questioned the
trembling and half-conscious Edgar. Edgar was sick
and could hardly speak. But he managed to say the
name of Joseph Snodgrass, the editor of the *Baltimore
Saturday Visiter*. Walker quickly scribbled a note:

> Dear Sir,
> There is a gentleman, rather the worse for
> wear, at Ryan's 4th ward polls, who goes
> under the [name] of Edgar A. Poe, and
> who appears in great distress, and he says
> he is acquainted with you, and I assure
> you he is in need of immediate assistance.
> Yours, in haste,
> [Joseph] W. Walker

Snodgrass hurried over to where Edgar was.
He found Edgar inside a tavern, helplessly confused
and sick in an armchair. His hair was messy. His
clothes were dirty and ragged.

COOPING

When Edgar was found on Election Day in Baltimore, he wasn't wearing his own clothes. Some people suspect that Edgar was the victim of "cooping." At this time, political gangs tried to make sure their candidate was elected any way they could. One method was to kidnap people and hold them in a room (the "coop"). The gangs would beat them and force them to go to the polls to vote several times. The victims' clothing would be changed to avoid the possibility of the voters being recognized at the polls.

Henry Herring, the husband of Maria Clemm's sister, arrived soon after Snodgrass. The two men checked Edgar into the Washington Medical College. Dr. John J. Moran, who admired Edgar's writing, examined the patient. Nurses and other hospital workers stopped their work to glance into the room. They also knew Edgar from his mysterious stories. They all watched as Edgar talked to the walls and windows. He couldn't control the shaking of his arms and legs. His vacant eyes sank back into his sickly, white face.

For three days, Edgar drifted in and out of consciousness. Dr. Moran could do little more than keep his patient comfortable. While Edgar was in the hospital, no one told Maria in New

York. His friends in Richmond had no idea either. As far as his friends and family knew, Edgar had just disappeared.

Early on Sunday, October 7, 1849, Edgar started shouting the name *Reynolds* over and over. The bewildered nurses and Dr. Moran tried to quiet him. Jeremiah Reynolds was the name of a real-life Antarctic explorer. Edgar had used Reynolds's voyage to the South Pole to write *The Narrative of Arthur Gordon Pym.* In Edgar's book, the explorer drifts helplessly toward the white mists and icy Antarctic waters that meant death.

Finally, just a few hours later, forty-year-old Edgar Allan Poe stopped his strange chant. He suddenly woke up and whispered, "Lord help my poor soul!" Then he died.

FAMOUS IN DEATH

On October 9, 1849, Edgar was buried in the Presbyterian Cemetery of Baltimore. The Reverend W. T. D. Clemm gave a funeral service to a small group. Twenty-six years later, Edgar's body was moved to a new grave in the same cemetery. He lies beside the bodies of his wife Virginia and of Maria Clemm.

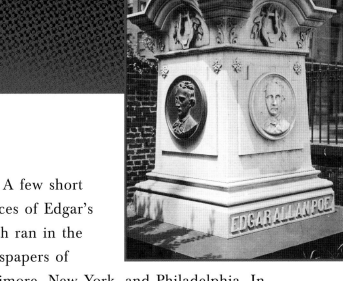

Edgar's tomb in Baltimore

A few short notices of Edgar's death ran in the newspapers of Baltimore, New York, and Philadelphia. In Richmond, newspaper and journal editors wrote long and admiring articles. To them, Edgar was a son of the South, a man of talent and deep sentiments. He stood out as an alternative to the cold and logical writers of the North. The cities of Philadelphia, Baltimore, and Richmond raised memorials to Edgar. Each city proudly claimed him as one of their own. Devoted readers made trips to Edgar's grave in the Presbyterian Cemetery.

IT'S A FACT!

Edgar's death notice in the *New York Tribune* was sent in anonymously. One of his main rivals, Rufus Griswold, wrote it. The notice praised Edgar's writing but not his character. Other writers publicly defended Poe in response.

After his death, Edgar gained a wide audience in foreign countries. The French poet Charles Baudelaire translated Edgar's stories and poems. Baudelaire's work made Edgar the most popular U.S. author in France. British writers also admired Edgar. The French detective C. Auguste Dupin—who appeared in "The Murders in the Rue Morgue" and two other stories—had a strong influence on Sir Arthur Conan Doyle. Doyle would borrow many of Dupin's traits to create his own fictional sleuth, Sherlock Holmes. By the end of the 1800s, readers in Spain, Germany, Russia, Italy, Portugal, and other nations were enjoying Edgar's stories and poetry.

Edgar grew even more popular in the 1900s. His horror stories found a worldwide audience. Teachers assigned Edgar's stories and poems to their students. Hollywood directors created scary films of "The Fall of the House of Usher" and "The Pit and the Pendulum." Edgar's name became closely tied to horror stories.

Many modern readers sympathize with Edgar's struggles. They see themselves in his search for fame and his feelings of isolation. His terrifying ghosts, gloomy castles, and grim tombs still fascinate them. Even more, they enjoy his exploration of the fears and desires of the human mind. It's as if the long-dead writer himself were sitting close by, whispering to them from within his quiet, marble tomb.

MEDIA DARLING

Edgar's life and work have never been forgotten. Performers have found ways to honor him. Operas and musicals have told his life story. Songs by the Beatles, Joan Baez, and Blues Traveler mention him or his work. The television show *The Simpsons* has used Edgar's poems. Both "The Raven" and "The Tell-Tale Heart" have been part of several episodes. In fact, the plot of "The Tell-Tale Head" was entirely based on the similarly named poem.

For mystery writers, there's no greater award than to receive an Edgar Allan Poe Award, or an Edgar. These awards are given each year to honor the best new mystery fiction, nonfiction, films, and TV shows. Awards are given in twelve categories including Best Novel, Best Short Story, Best Fact Crime, Best Children's Mystery, Best Motion Picture Screenplay, and Best Play.

bankrupt: unable to pay debts

boardinghouse: a place where people pay to live and get meals

customs house: a government building where taxes are collected and where ships are given permission to enter or leave the country

foster father: a man with whom a child legally lives but to whom the child is not related

narrator: in a novel or short story or poem, the person telling the story

the North: in the United States, the states that fought against the Confederacy (or South) in the Civil War (1861–1865)

prose: ordinary language used for speaking or writing

the South: in the United States, the states that fought against the Union (or North) in the Civil War (1861–1865)

stage fright: anxiety about performing in front of an audience

tuberculosis: a disease that is easy to catch and that usually affects the lungs. The illness was hard to cure in Edgar's time. These days, drugs can fully cure a person with the disease.

SOURCE NOTES

4–5   Edgar Allan Poe, "The Black
      Cat," *United States Saturday Post*,
      August 19, 1843.

21   John Ward Ostrom, ed., *The
      Letters of Edgar Allan Poe* (New
      York: Gordian Press, 1966),
      7–8.

54   Edgar Allan Poe, *Selected
      Writings of Edgar Allan Poe*,
      edited with an introduction by
      David Galloway (New York:
      Penguin Books, 1977), 138.

69   Ibid., 277.

70   Ibid., 282.

74   Ibid., 77–80.

100   Arthur Hobson Quinn, *Edgar
       Allan Poe: A Critical Biography*
       (Baltimore: Johns Hopkins
       Press, 1998), 638.

SELECTED BIBLIOGRAPHY

Allen, Hervey Israfel. *The Life and Times of Edgar Allan Poe.* New York: Farrar and Rinehart, 1934.

Anderson, Madelyn Klein. *Edgar Allan Poe: A Mystery.* New York: Franklin Watts, 1993.

Bittner, William. *Poe: A Biography.* Boston: Little, Brown, 1962.

Buranelli, Vincent. *Edgar Allan Poe.* Twayne's United States Authors series. Boston: Twayne Publishers, 1977.

The Cambridge History of American Literature. New York: Macmillan Company, 1943.

Canby, Henry Seidel. *Classic Americans: A Study of Eminent American Writers from Irving to Whitman.* New York: Russell and Russell, 1959.

Jacobs, William Jay. *Edgar Allan Poe: Genius in Torment.* New York: McGraw-Hill, 1975.

Knapp, Bettina. *Edgar Allan Poe.* New York: F. Unger, 1984.

LeVert, Suzanne. *Edgar Allan Poe.* Philadelphia: Chelsea House, 1992.

Loewen, Nancy. *Poe.* Mankato, MN: Creative Education, 1993.

Mankowitz, Wolf. *The Extraordinary Mr. Poe.* New York: Summit Books, 1978.

Ostrom, John Ward, ed. *The Letters of Edgar Allan Poe.* New York: Gordian Press, 1966.

Poe, Edgar Allan. *The Other Poe: Comedies and Satires.* Edited with an introduction by David Galloway. New York: Penguin Books, 1983.

Poe, Edgar Allan. *Selected Writings of Edgar Allan Poe.* Edited with an introduction by David Galloway. New York: Penguin Books, 1977.

Quinn, Arthur Hobson. *Edgar Allan Poe: A Critical Biography.* Baltimore: Johns Hopkins Press, 1998.

Shorto, Russell. *Edgar Allan Poe: Creator of Dreams.* New York: Kipling Press, 1988.

Silverman, Kenneth. *Edgar A. Poe: Mournful and Never-Ending Remembrance.* New York: HarperCollins, 1991.

Stem, Philip Van Doren. *Edgar Allan Poe, Visitor from the Night of Time.* New York: Crowell, 1973.

FURTHER READING AND WEBSITES

Avi. *The Man Who Was Poe.* New York: HarperTrophy, 1997.

The Edgar Allan Poe Society of Baltimore
http://www.eapoe.org
The website of the Edgar Allan Poe Society of Baltimore gives details about his life and links to places to visit.

The House of Usher
http://www.houseofusher.net
This cool website lists films and comic books based on Poe's works. Links help students with research papers about Poe's work.

Kent, Zachary. *Edgar Allan Poe: Tragic Poet and Master of Mystery.* Springfield, NJ: Enslow Publishers, 2001.

Peltak, Jennifer. *Edgar Allan Poe.* New York: Chelsea House Publications, 2004.

Poe, Edgar Allan. *Tales of Mystery and Madness.* New York: Atheneum, 2004.

Poe, Edgar Allan. *Tales of Mystery and Terror.* Mankato, MN: Abdo Publishing Company, 2002.

The Poe Decoder
http://www.poedecoder.com
This website gives a background on Poe's works. It also has links to some of the more useful Poe sites.

PHOTO ACKNOWLEDGMENTS

The images in this book are used with the permission of: © Brown Brothers, pp. 6, 45, 78, 81 (left); Harvard Theatre Collection, The Houghton Library, p. 7; Courtesy of the Edgar Allan Poe Museum, Richmond, Virginia, p. 9 (left), 36, 43; Valentine Richmond History Center, p. 9 (right); The Library of Virginia, p. 10; Collection of The New-York Historical Society, 19745, p. 12; The Lilly Library, Indiana University, Bloomington, IN, p. 17; © MPI/Getty Images, pp. 18, 23; © CORBIS, p. 24; © North Wind Picture Archives, pp. 30, 32, 55, 79, 86, 93; © Bettmann/CORBIS, pp. 34, 35, 61, 69; Print Collection, Miriam and Ira D. Wallach Division of Art, Prints and Photographs, The New York Public Library, Astor, Lenox and Tilden Foundations, p. 49; Courtesy Fales Library, New York University, p. 51; National Archives, pp. 11, (NWDNS-111-96967), 52 (NWDNS-111-B-4202); Society Portrait Collection, The Historical Society of Pennsylvania, p. 59; Library of Congress (HABS, PA, 51-PHILA, 663A), p. 72; © Hulton Archive/ Getty Images, p. 81 (right); © Rischgitz/Getty Images, p. 94; Cook Collection, Valentine Richmond History Center, p. 98; © Authenticated News/Getty Images, p. 103.

Cover: © Rischgitz/Getty Images.